Coin

The Irreverent Yet Practical Guide to Money Management for Recent College Graduates

Judy McNary, CFP®

With Illustrations by Jenna Kusmierek

Direct inquiries for volume purchases to the publisher, Sunny Money, LLC, at www.coininthebank.com

ISBN:

ISBN-13: 978-0-9888519-0-0

What readers are saying about <u>Coin</u>

"Every college grad should be given this book with their diploma. It's a great guide to making smart money choices." - **Jill Gianola, CFP®, Owner, Gianola Financial Planning and author of The Young Couples Guide to Growing Rich Together.**

"I was stoked to find a book that so concisely and humorously laid out all the pieces of the financial quagmire that is real life. I think I won't have to live in a box now despite my Humanities degree." - **Jack D.**

"Spot on." – **Brian P.**

"Most money management books have little to say to newly-minted college grads. With Coin, Judy McNary gives the younger set an entertaining, colorful workbook that will help them map out their own path to prosperity."– **David Gardner, CFP®, Personal Finance Columnist, Boulder Daily Camera.**

"... it was absolutely hilarious. The knowledge is basic enough for even the most financially inept person but still engaging enough for someone with more financial understanding." – **Alicia R.**

"'As a financial planner & mother of 3, I think it's important we do everything we can to get young adults started on solid financial ground. I've given a copy of this book to my son, Dallas, and I hope he reads it." - **Linda Leitz, CFP®, Owner, It's Not Just Money, Inc and author of We Need to Talk: Money & Kids After Divorce.**

"I read it – it's nice that it's short. I liked it. I got a lot out of it." - **Dallas L.**

"Accounting and Finance are always the classes that students seem to hate. I would love to give my classmates this book. They would learn more in 88 pages than in 16 weeks of class. - **Brenna B.**

"Coin is terrific; I've ordered a copy for each of my clients." - **Penny Marchand, CFP®, Principal, Cambridge Financial Group.**

"I found the chapter on student loan debt very helpful. I think that this is an area that a lot of recent graduates are concerned about. I absolutely loved the humor and sassiness of the book." – **Betsy G.**

Dedication

To Tom, Jack, and Erin,
from whom I learn so much.
You make my life rich.
To Scott,
it's a grand life we have.

And,
to the youth of America,
I believe your future's so bright
you're gonna need shades.

Table of Contents

Acknowledgements

Thank you to the brave young men and women who suffered through early versions of this book and boldly let me know when something was totally lame. Thanks also to those I've met over the years who shared their monetary fears and frustrations. Your stories inspired me to want to make a difference.

Coin (koin) n.

1. *flat round chunk of metal used to buy stuff*
2. *slang term for money*
3. *the personal finance book used by successful college graduates*

Why Read This?

*B*ecause it's about money. And it doesn't matter whether you love it or hate it—you need to be smart about it. Manage your money well and life is good, but mess it up and suddenly life sucks. And if you don't fix it, you could end up old and poor. And bitter. And we don't want that.

<u>Coin</u> takes you step by step through the basics so you'll understand your finances and not stress about them. It keeps you from making expensive mistakes. It helps you recover from mistakes you may have already made. It's funny. It's short. It has pictures. It's a chapter book. ~~It's cheap~~. It's a "good value." You get to write all over it. Did I mention it's short? Invest just two hours reading cover to cover and you'll know what you need to be financially smart. You'll have a plan. And you'll have fun doing it. I absolutely guarantee it.*

As our cover man Ben famously said, "Time is money." So, grab a pen, pencil, or crayon, and let's get started.

There is a slight chance this may not be true, but you've got the book so go ahead and give it a whirl..

Quiz: Test Your Money IQ

You thought finishing college meant no more tests? You thought wrong. Sorry. Life is actually just one test after another. See how you do on this true/false quiz.

_____ 1. People enjoy hanging out with people who complain about how broke they are all the time.

_____ 2. People who can manage their money wisely have way better sex lives than those who don't.

_____ 3. Always exercise caution when opening the overhead bins because items may have shifted during flight.

Answers: 1. False 2. True 3. True

What's the Money For?

"You have brains in your head. You have feet in your shoes. You can steer yourself any direction you choose."
~ Dr. Seuss, Oh, the Places You'll Go!

We begin with figuring out what you want your money to do for you. That's right—it's your money. What do you want to do with it? Maybe you're all about thrill-a-minute outdoor adventure travel. Perhaps mundane-but-rewarding freedom-from-debt is what will make you fulfilled. How about a little of each? It's your money and your life.

Spend the next few minutes writing down what you want in life. I'm talking about your goals. Big ones, small ones, crazy ones. Let 'em fly. Have fun here. Maybe you really want to buy a new car. Or climb Denali. Get out of debt. Backpack through Thailand. Learn to play slide guitar. Go to grad school. Rollerblade down Machu Picchu. Well, maybe not that. How about achieving financial freedom? That sounds kind of cool, doesn't it? Don't get hung up on whether you think your goals are realistic or not. For now, just write them down, and we'll worry about the details later. Start the clock—you've got 10 minutes. On your mark, get set, go.

Goals

Today's Date: _____

1. _____
2. _____
3. _____
4. _____
5. _____
6. _____
7. _____
8. _____
9. *Emergency Fund* _____
10. *Financial Freedom* _____

Now you have a glorious list o' goals. This should have you pretty energized, right? Keep adding more as they pop into your head. Writing goals down helps make them real. Feel free to draw pictures or doodle in the margins.

Your next step is to prioritize your goals. I absolutely want you to aim big and high—but we can't take on everything at once. So we need to dial in on just a few goals to start. In the margin next to Emergency Fund, write #1. In ink. I've got dibs on this because your first priority *must* be to establish an emergency fund. I'll explain what this is in the next chapter. For now, just accept this as your most immediate goal. Priorities for the rest are up to you. Go ahead and put an order number next to each.

What are your top three? These are the goals we're going to focus on first. Once you have a plan for these, we'll work on the others.

The Top Three

1. *Emergency Fund*
2.
3.

The Coin Jar

You need to have a coin jar. It can be a piggy bank, an old jug-wine bottle, or a flea-market special. Keep out what you need for laundry, but faithfully add the rest of your spare change to the jar. This money is for your big, crazy goals.

3 Coin in the Bank

"A little magic can take you a long way."
~ Roald Dahl, Charlie and the Chocolate Factory

op priority for your money is saving some of it. Why? Because you've got dreams and goals. Big ones. And the easiest way to reach those goals is by following the Platinum Rule.

The Platinum Rule
SPEND LESS THAN YOU MAKE

Platinum?
What's that about?
Well, the Golden Rule was already taken (duh) and silver tarnishes so that wasn't going to work. Bronze? Nah—not shiny enough. But seriously, platinum is cool stuff. It's rare and has so many amazing properties it's quite valuable. Just like this rule. Practice the Platinum Rule and life is good.

Yup, it's that simple. Spend less money than you make. Why does it seem so hard? Because unless you do something radical like go live off the grid, you are bombarded by opportunities to spend your hard-earned coin. Things you just gotta have, like Zombie Plush Slippers or a virtual iThing.

Quick now—flash back to fourth grade when you played Mad Libs® at a slumber party. Go ahead and fill in the blanks below.

But don't worry. I'm not saying you can't ever buy a sleek, candy-apple red
_____ or shop for a _____ plaid_____.
         NOUN   *COLOR*   *NOUN*

What I am saying is that you need to wait to buy things until you've set aside a portion of what you earn. This is what's known as paying yourself first. For starters, you should save at least 10% of your income. More if you've laid out some truly audacious goals.

Let's walk through a simple example. Throughout this book when I'm talking about your income or your salary, I am referring to your gross salary. Gross is the amount before taxes and other deductions are taken out. And yes, taxes are gross. You know, Ben Franklin once said we all need to handle humor as well as our finances.* Moving on.

What if you don't have a job?

If you don't have a job, you don't have income. Put this book down. Your first job is to get a job. Any job. Don't worry about finding one in your field. You're young — you have many years to work in your field, your meadow, or even your glen. Right now you need to find a way to earn money. Once you've got that, pick up this book right where you left off. I'll wait.

Your salary is $3,000 per month.

Your savings formula: $3,000 X

10% = $300

At the very least, you should save $300 per month.

What if your paychecks vary? You're a nurse and night shifts pay more. Or you're

Ben may not have actually said that, but I know he would've said it if he'd thought of it.

in sales and you get commissions every other paycheck. You do project work and some months you get paid more than others. You're a waiter and most of your pay is tips. Don't make this hard—just take the average.

> **Your Total Savings Per Month**
> **Your monthly salary:**_____
> **Your monthly savings formula:** _____ **x 10% =** _____

Easiest way to make this happen? Set up auto-transfer each pay period from your checking to your savings account so you never see it. Then keep your hands off. Remember—10% is the *minimum*. Aim higher to reach your goals sooner.

In Case of Emergency

The first thing to use your savings for is to build an emergency fund. It's pretty much exactly what it sounds like—a pot of money set aside for emergencies. Emergencies are unexpected financial whammies like cars breaking down or accidents that rack up medical bills. To be financially sound you have to have an emergency fund. Period. Here's how much you need:

Monthly income: _____ **x three months =** _____

I know that sounds like a lot if you're starting from zero but I need you to get there as quickly as you can. Think about it. What would you do if you lose your job or have an accident while hang gliding? Your emergency fund keeps you from having to sleep on the street. Seriously. It buys you time to find a new job or put all those broken bones back in the right places. It's for flying back to Colorado for the funeral because they killed Kenny. Those _____.

NOUN

This money needs to stay put, though. No emergency, no touchy. It belongs in a *savings* account—not checking. You want access to the money when you're in dire straits, but you do not want to be tempted by it. Build it and forget about it.

Set the date: *I will have my emergency fund in place by*
_____ / _____ / _____

Avoid the Tidal Savings Trap

If you have to keep tapping your savings to cover expenses each month, they're not
SAVINGS! Once money goes into savings, it stays in. Not in and out and in and out like
the tide. Except for real emergencies. And we're not talking about fixing a botched
dye job. Well, actually that could be an emergency, depending on how bad the dye job
really is. Anyway, if you're starting from zero and cleaning up a financial mess or two,
you can begin by saving a smaller percentage of your income—say 3 or 4 percent, then
increase it every three months until you're at the target savings rate of 10 percent.

Hurry up and start saving because once you have your emergency fund in place, you get to start chasing all the exciting entries on your goals list—the trip to Amsterdam, the Volkl Gotamas, the new set of wheels...

Quiz: Emergency Fund

Which is an appropriate reason to tap your emergency fund?

A. BFF Jessica called and Nordstrom's has a sale on Kate Spade purses.

B. Alpha Sig brother Louie called and is in jail in Las Vegas after a night a la The Hangover. He needs bail money.

C. Your car is leaking oil. The auto repair guy says the rear main is toast. You need that car for work.

D. The airlines have launched a fare war - half off tickets to Cancun.

E. You want to have surgery to close the gauge holes in your earlobes.

Answers:
A & D are wrong. Use other money for these-not the emergency fund.
B. Have Louie call his folks instead. They love this kind of stuff.
C. Yeah, we'll accept this. Most dads would, too.
E. Absolutely. It's about time.
Give yourself a star or a smiley face if you chose answer C or E.

4 Debt

"I didn't fail the test, I just found 100 ways to do it wrong."
~ Ben Franklin

ebt — ugh. Amazing how four little letters can pack such a wallop. What a buzz kill. Here we were, having a perfectly fine time talking about goals and such, and I have to go and bring up debt. Why? Because the sooner you deal with it, the happier you will be. Trust me. Debt-annihilation has to be part of your plan or you won't be able to reach those great goals you've got.

I'll let you in on a secret: Avoid debt. If you want something, save for it. When you've saved enough, then buy it. This is kind of a corollary to the Platinum Rule we introduced in the previous chapter. I would love to take full credit for this powerful concept but I can't because I didn't invent it. Neither did Al Gore. The Platinum Rule works. For real. Deferred gratification may not sound as fun as instant gratification but independent studies* show it lasts longer, tastes great, and is less filling.

All well and good, you say, but maybe your "no-debt horse" already left the barn. (That's old-people speak for "it's a little late now.") Those 3 AM pizzas you had delivered during finals, the cute shoes you wore to the Omega Nu spring formal,

*Both people I asked agreed that this is true.

and yeah, a chunk of Spring Break Mazatlan - complete with the commemorative shot glass - have done a number on your credit cards. Even if you're not maxed out, you know you need to get rid of all that debt.

Here's how to get started. Fill in the chart below with current balances on everything you owe. Don't put your student loans here - we're going to take them on in the next chapter. And if you don't have any debt, that makes things easy, doesn't it? Give yourself a pat on the back, take a short break, and skip on down to the Credit Cards section.

Here's an example:

Type of Debt	Amount You Owe	Interest Rate	Monthly Payment	Date Paid Off	Lender
Credit Card	1,800	18.9%	62	–	Kapital2
Personal Loan	2,500	1%	100	2015	Bank O' Mom & Dad
TOTAL	**4,300**		162		

Now it's your turn:

Type of Debt	Amount You Owe	Interest Rate	Monthly Payment	Date Paid Off	Lender
TOTAL					

Next, we calculate your consumer debt-to-income ratio. Add up just the credit cards, car loans, and other consumer debt. (Remember we're going to deal with your student loans in the next chapter.) Plug the numbers into the equation below.

Example:

$$\frac{\textbf{Total Consumer Debt}}{\textbf{Your Annual Income}} = \frac{\$4,300}{\$35,000} = 12.3\%$$

Your Turn:

$$\frac{\textbf{Total Consumer Debt}}{\textbf{Your Annual Income}} = \underline{\hspace{2cm}} =$$

Assess Your Results

A+ *So sweet*

Trust me – just ask one of your debt-laden comrades if you're not sure you appreciate how good life is. They'll tell you. 0%

A *Excellent* 1-10%

Just pay down that bit you've got. If you don't have your Emergency Fund yet, pay down your debt and build the fund in parallel.

12-20% B *Pretty good*

Clean up required but manageable. Don't take on any additional debt. Hold off on your spending until you get below the 10% mark. If you don't have your Emergency Fund yet, pay down your debt and build the fund in parallel.

C *Yikes!*

Cut up those cards; your top priority is to get your debt/income ratio down to the teens. Pay for everything with cash. Stay away from Internet shopping sites! Double up on payments – get moving. Pay off the debt with highest interest rates fastest. Try to make a small contribution to your Emergency Fund each month – even $25 or $50 but your focus needs to be on getting your debt under control. Do not take on additional debt of any sort. Seriously.

21-40%

F *Ouch*

This is a rough one. I hope you at least had fun while racking up this mountain of owe. Same recommendations as for C-debtors except hold off on the Emergency Fund. Get a second job. Move back home. Tackle this aggressively before it balloons further or you could end up living in a box. Under a bridge. Not smelling very good.

>41%

Credit Cards

Despite the bad press, the warnings, and the headlines, most of you will find it's a good idea to have a credit card. Look at all the good things magic plastic can do for you.

Top Ten Reasons To Have A Credit Card:

1. **Flexibility.** Road-tripping and need gas in Elko, Nevada at 2 AM? Fill 'er up.
2. **Protection.** Lose the card and all you need to do is call some phone number to report it. The credit card company then cancels the card and you won't be liable for items the thief purchased. Lose cash, on the other hand, and you're SOL.
3. **Product and service purchase guarantees.** If you didn't get what you paid for, your credit card company steps up to the plate with you to settle the dispute with the merchant.
4. **Ease of travel.** Buy plane tickets, reserve hotel rooms, and rent cars using credit cards. Planning ahead a little keeps you from sleeping on park benches, you know.
5. **Ease of international travel.** Even better. You don't have to spend half your vacation converting your bucks to bahts and back again.
6. **Earn points.** For miles, cool stuff, more miles, and sometimes cold, hard cash.
7. **Establish a credit history.** This will show you pay bills on time. Did you catch that? Let me repeat it - you want it to show you pay your bills on time. Otherwise, of course, you're hosed.
8. **Business expense reimbursement.** If you travel or buy supplies for your job, using a credit card means you can make the purchase, submit your expense report to your employer, and get reimbursed before the credit card bill is due. Keeps your personal cash-flow flowing.
9. **Free borrowing.** As long as you don't screw up and forget to pay it off in full every month. Remember that. You need to pay it off in full every month. One more time. Pay it off every month.
10. **Lightweight.** Fits perfectly in your wallet (how did they know?) or jeans pocket.

How many credit cards should you have? **One.** Get one card and pay it in full every month. If you travel for work, get a second card and use that strictly for business expenses. Credit cards are like brownies. One brownie is good, two might be good if you're incredibly hungry, but attack a whole pan and you'll experience seriously diminishing marginal returns. Too much of a good thing is NOT a good thing.

Establishing Your Credit History

Your credit history is a report that shows all the debt and/or credit cards you've ever had and how well you did at paying it all back. No debt = no credit history. You have your whole life to establish a credit history. No urgency here. Banks and credit card companies encourage you to build a credit history because when you borrow money they make money. It's kind of like those Hallmark card holidays. Let's play a little Mad Libs® again.

Hallmark makes "Happy _____, _____!" cards and wants you to feel
HOLIDAY   OBSCURE RELATIVE
guilty if you don't send one to every _____.
SAME OBSCURE RELATIVE

After you graduate, practice living within your means. Follow The Platinum Rule. Spend less than you make. Get one credit card for convenience. Pay it off promptly, always. You honestly don't need to do anything else for the first couple years out of school.

Top Reason Not To Have A Credit Card

There is one reason credit cards get all the bad press, the warnings, and the headlines.

1. **Overspending.** If you can't say no to buying, do yourself a huge favor and hold off getting a credit card. Use cash, checks, and a debit card. Memorize the Platinum Rule. Make it your mantra. Spend less than you make. Make sure you know where your money is going. Remember, it's not the credit card - it's your spending, silly.

Be Part of the 35%

Only 35% of all credit card holders pay their cards off every month. Make sure you are one of them.

How to Build Credit the Easy Way

Here's the deal:

1. Track your spending. Your goal is to spend less money than you're making. This is The _____ Rule.
   PRECIOUS METAL
2. After you spend less than you earn for three months, get a gas card.*
3. Use the gas card once a month and pay it off immediately.
4. After you've had the gas card for at least three months and you've paid it off each month on time, go for a general credit card like a Visa, MasterCard, or Discover.
5. Sign up for one with no annual fees and low interest rates.

6. Use your shiny new piece o' plastic once or twice a month. Pay the entire bill each month. Always.

7. Don't date anyone who thinks this is stupid. Otherwise, before you know it, you'll be paying for everything - all the concerts, the bar tabs, the meals. And then who's the stupid one?

If you don't drive replace "gas" with "store with stuff you really don't like." Gals, think Cabela's. Guys, think Linens-N-Things. The goal here is to wade into the credit card waters carefully. That means getting a card you won't use much.

How many credit card offers will you receive weekly? Way too many.

Just because someone offers you something doesn't mean you should take it. Shred the offers but mail back the empty postage-paid envelopes - just for sport.

5 Oh Crap More Debt

"An investment in knowledge always pays the best interest."
~ Ben Franklin

Student loans are such a fun topic that they've earned the right to a chapter of their own. That's a lie. Student loans are not a fun topic at all. If it were up to me, I'd be jumping right in to funding ski trips, concert tickets, or chocolate Labrador Retriever puppies. No, student loans have their own chapter because there are over one trillion dollars' worth of them in this country and that's too big a number to ignore. These loans get in the way of what you can spend on housing, transportation, food, and junk, so if you've got 'em, repaying them needs to be a core part of your plan. If you do not have student loans, great - bounce on ahead to the next chapter. But if you do, read on.

First things first. Since misery loves company, I recommend you use your 140-character communication talent to get the word out for an official Student Loan Commiseration Night*. Wear your school colors. Laugh, dance, butcher some karaoke, or just kick back and relax. Going to college was a good move. The debt? Well, it is what it is.

---

*Please don't call it this. Come up with something fun so people will actually come.

All right, let's put the plan in place. Your loans come with a grace period. You generally have six months after you finish school before you have to start making loan payments. Use the grace period to build your Emergency Fund. Don't put it off. You know the slogan: Just do it. You'll thank me later. Set your starting point by filling out the first three columns of the loan table.

Here's an example:

Lender	Amount You Owe	Interest Rate	Monthly Payment	Date Paid Off
Plus Loan	$15,000	6.8%		
First Bank of Gotham	$10,000	Variable		
TOTAL	**$25,000**			

Now here's yours:

Lender	Amount You Owe	Interest Rate	Monthly Payment	Date Paid Off
TOTAL				

How you go about repaying student loans varies, depending on whether they are private or federal loans. For federal loans, it also depends on your expected earning power and the total amount you owe. Ready, set, here we go.

Private Loans

Not all private loans are created equal, but there are some general options you can expect to see.

1. **Repayment term:** You will choose how long you want to take to pay back the loan. If you select a longer term, say 20 years instead of 15, your payments generally will be smaller. But you'll end up paying more over the life of the loan. And, if you have a variable rate loan, those smaller payments aren't guaranteed. If the rate goes up, the payments go up.
2. **Rate:** Variable or fixed. If you're willing to gamble on rates, you'll start out with a lower interest rate than if you lock in the fixed rate for your loan. If you have borrowed a small amount and plan to pay your loan(s) off quickly, you end up paying less interest with the variable rate than the fixed rate. If you're not sure, you might be better off locking in the fixed rate. Then you know exactly what you owe every month until that loan is history.

3. **Consolidation:** Not consolation - consolidation. No consoling here. If you have more than one loan, lenders will offer you the chance to combine them. And you get to choose from a new menu of repayment terms, rates, and other toppings. Look at consolidating if the rates on all your loans are about the same. Don't do it if you've got a couple low-rate loans, because you lose those low rates when all the loans get mushed together.

Now, let's walk through an example with the $10,000 we borrowed from the First Bank of Gotham. If you're willing to take a chance on the variable rate, you'll start with smaller payments. Remember, the rates can change and your payments can end up much bigger than the current fixed-rate option.

Repayment Term*	Fixed/Variable Rate	Monthly Payment
15 years	Fixed at 6.99%	$118.07
15 years	Variable at 3.5% to 9.99%	$82.74 to $155.67

*Term includes 4 year deferment while in school

Federal Loans

Most of your loans are probably federal loans. These come in more flavors, but there are some basic guidelines that apply to your options for repaying them.

1. **Standard repayment:** You pay the loan back in 10 years. You make the same payment every month. After 10 years or 120 payments, your loan is paid in full. If I were you, this is the option I'd take. Gut it out for 10 years and be done with it. The time will pass faster than you think. Just ask anyone over the age of 35.
2. **Extended repayment:** If you owe more than $30,000, you can opt to take up to 25 years to pay it back through fixed payments or graduated payments. (Graduated payments start out smaller and bump up every two years.) At the end of the 25 years, you'll have completely paid off the loan. Hopefully, you'll still have all your teeth so you can smile when you're done!
3. **Consolidation:** This one gets a little sticky, so stay with me. And again, we're

not consoling, we're consolidating. Big difference. As discussed in the private-loan section, with this option, you merge all your loans into one. Depending on how much you owe, you can take more time to pay the debt back and you can go with fixed or graduated payments.

Amount	$7,500-9,999	$10,000 - $19,999	$20,000 - $39,999	$40,000 - $59,000	$60,000 or more
Years to Pay Back	12	15	20	25	30

4. **Income-based repayment (aka "IBR"):** Not to be confused with PBR, IBR is a relatively new option that continues to undergo Congressional refinements. Basically, IBR attempts to keep your annual payment low enough in relation to your annual income that you don't completely starve while you're paying back your loans. Your diet may still be heavily ramen-and-PBR-based, but spice things up with a little lunch meat every once in a while and you'll be fine. In financialese, IBR caps your annual payment at 10% of your adjusted gross income (AGI) minus 150% of the federal poverty line. Faithfully make these payments month in and month out, and after 25 years if you still owe money, the balance of the debt is forgiven. You're done. Of course, it's not quite as simple as that. As your income goes up over the years, the payment increases so that, at some point, you may make too much to qualify for IBR. In that case, you'll get switched over to the extended-repayment or consolidation programs. All the interest you didn't pay, because you couldn't afford it, gets tacked on to the total amount you owe. If you bounce along with low income for 25 years and do end up qualifying for loan forgiveness, you have to pay income tax on the amount forgiven. Which kind of sucks. So, if you're broke, you've got a mountain of student loan debt, and you've got a job that doesn't pay squat, start with IBR and transition to one of the other programs as soon as your income allows.

5. **Public Service Loan Forgiveness:** PSLF is yet another option that might work for you. First, to be eligible, you've got to work for a federal, state, or local government, a tax-exempt non-profit, or a qualifying public-service organization that is actually a private non-profit employer. Think public

library, law enforcement, public health. Next, you've got to be employed full-time, which generally means at least 30 hours per week. Teachers, check out your contracts - you may qualify if you work at least 30 hours per week during the contract period. And if you have two qualifying jobs that together get you over the 30 hours per week, that can count, too. Okay, now, what you do is make 120 regular full monthly payments on your student loans. If don't miss a single one and you stay employed full time in the public sector for an entire decade, whatever's left on the loans is forgiven. No taxes due. Pretty cool, right? If you go this route, make sure you never miss a single loan payment and that you stay employed the entire time or you're toast. Could be a great option if you take the extended repayment plan.

6. **Other stuff:** Depending on your profession, you might qualify for grants that will reduce or eliminate some of your student loan debt. They all have very specific criteria, so do your homework. Check out AmeriCorps, Teach for America, and the Peace Corps to see if any of these work for your situation.

Are your eyes completely glazed over? Yeah, mine are too. Here's what I recommend: First, absolutely do not miss payments (default) on your student loans. The frumious student loan Bandersnatch will hunt you down and when he finds you, it's not pretty. We don't want that. Second, pay as aggressively as you can afford to. The longer you take to pay these loans, the more interest you'll pay and the longer it will be before you can spend money on more fun things. If you qualify and need to start small to be able to eat, then start small. When your overall financial situation gets better, put more toward paying off your loans. Pay attention to federal legislation about repayment of student loans. Every couple years, new options are added. One just might come along that makes your life better.

What about graduate school? Yes, you can defer payment on your student loans

> ### 3 Tips for Tackling Student Loan Debt
>
> 1. Stay current on all your loans - always.
> 2. Pay off loans with higher interest rates faster.
> 3. Each month, challenge yourself to pay more than you did the month before. Little bits add up for big impact. Chip away at that principal.

while you are in grad school. But - and it's a big "but" here - do not go to grad school simply because you believe you will come out and earn BIG bucks. I'll make an exception for those of you who know you're going to become surgeons or work in some similarly lucrative field. Apply to grad school, get accepted, then work your tail off by any legal means possible. Save to pay for as much of grad school as possible before you start. If it means you defer for a year, then do that.

Money Manners

You share everything with the world. Your friends. Your celebrations. Your thoughts. Your likes. Your dislikes.

Draw the line with sharing information on your debt. Money can really warp the way people think. Some types of information are best kept to your inner circle, and student-loan debt falls squarely into this category. Same goes for your salary. And don't ask people to share theirs with you. At best, it makes things awkward. At worst, it comes back to bite you.

6 Somewhere to Sleep

"Am I right or am I left?"
~ Roald Dahl, The BFG

You graduated from college. Excellent. You have a job. Well done. You can get a place of your own ~~yes!~~ Whoops, not so fast. Unless you are in one of those high-dollar-right-out-of-the-gate professions, you probably aren't going to be making enough money to afford a place of your own just yet.

Sorry for the letdown. Just when you thought the days of roommate horror stories were in your rearview mirror. You know what I'm talking about - everyone has at least one. The Slob. The Hog. The Super Slob Hog. The Perma-PMS Drama Queen. The Control Freak. The Flake. Or maybe just the garden-variety cheapskate who used all your Italian salad dressing when she thought you weren't looking. Twice. I could go on - when you're not living the roommate nightmare, it's kind of fun to write about, actually. But that's a different book.

Here's the number: Your total housing cost should be no more than 20-25% of your gross income. This includes utilities, such as electricity and gas, plus water and trash. If you have student loans, car loans, or credit cards to pay off, dial back further on housing. Same goes if you have big-ticket goals you want to accomplish - the more you spend on housing, the less you have for everything else. After all, it's just a place to sleep. Here's the formula:

> **Your Total Housing Allowance Per Month**
> Your monthly salary _____ x 20 - 25% = _____

For example, if you're earning **$3,000** a month, your rent plus utilities should run you no more than **$750**. If this puts you in a decent place in a safe neighborhood, then go ahead and sign the lease. On the other hand, if you aren't fortunate enough to be working in Harlingen, Texas or Pueblo, Colorado and you're stuck somewhere like San Francisco or Boston (sigh), you're going to have to look at other options.

Options for Cutting Down on Housing Costs

1. **Get a roommate.** Two live more cheaply than one. Use your previous experience with roommates to help you screen out what you do and don't like. They weren't always happy, but Ernie and Bert managed to work things out.
2. **Move back home for a bit.** If reading that sentence made your entire body shudder, then skip on down to number 3. If not, consider the pros and cons. Parents typically charge below-market rents. Seriously. They will give you a really good deal. Use the rent money you save to pay down your debts, pay off debt, or put aside for your own place. Just don't waste it. Please. This should be a limited-term engagement.
3. **Lengthen your commute.** If you expand your search radius, you'll increase your chances of finding a place you can afford. You'll be spending more time in transit, though, so don't forget to factor that into your overall budget.
4. **Lengthen your commute and get a roommate.** Or two.
5. **Find someone who needs an on-site house manager.** Look for a property owner who has a basement apartment, a pool house, or some other separate living space. In exchange for free or reduced rent, you can work out an arrangement to take care of the property.

If none of these options works, you're in a tough spot. I mean, there are a few other options, but I am trying to stick with legal, socially acceptable ones here. If you are a slave... oops, I mean, if you have an internship that doesn't pay money but is the only way to break into your chosen field, you probably need to wait tables or tend bar evenings and weekends to make it work. Selling SliceCo knives to your parents and all their friends is an option. Especially if you work the upsell. You know, where you innocuously suggest that if they order the next bigger set, today only, you could throw in the extra-special Kevlar® vegetable peeler. If that whole idea is repulsive, consider talking to your parents about a temporary subsidy. Just remember to repay their help later when you've made it big. If your job is a paying job but it doesn't pay you enough to live on, you might need to rethink the whole thing.

"What about real estate?" you ask. Please don't. Not yet. Don't buy real estate if you're just graduating from college. Before making a commitment to a mortgage, make sure you like your job and the area. If there's a 20 percent or greater chance in the next two years that you'll be moving cross country to live with your girlfriend/boyfriend, change climates, or get that MBA, don't buy anything yet. Wait until you are sure you're ready for the time and money sink that comes with home ownership.

If you're new to an area, spend at least a year there before committing to real estate. Maybe you love it the day you arrive, but over time you might discover you absolutely hate living where the bugs are the size of Chihuahuas. Or the stupid way everybody talks. Or the constant 90-mph winds, the blizzards, the months on end with no sun, the weeks of 90-90s, the lousy drivers, whatever. You get the idea.

The reverse is also true. When you first arrive, you might think you hate everything. Give it a year and you might decide you love it. You give each of the bugs a pet name, you adopt the local dialect, or you become a windsurfing maniac.

Either way, you'll be glad you waited.

No Rush on Home Ownership

Everyone knows the #1 rule of real estate is location, location, location. But few people know the #2 rule: Easy to buy, tough to sell. Owning real estate is a BIG commitment. You just graduated from college. Go ahead and frolic a little. You have plenty of time to build and feather your nest down the road.

Getting Around

"Buy the ticket, take the ride."
~ Hunter S. Thompson

There are two kinds of people in this world: those who need their own set of wheels to get around and those who don't. Which are you?

No Car

- You live in an area with good public transit. You can take a bus, a train, a ferry, the subway, or on special occasions, a taxi cab scented with *eau de b.o.*
- You've got a bike that you ride everywhere. You live in a climate, both physically and culturally, that makes this a great option.
- You're green. You bleed Kermit-the-Frog green. "No fossil fuels" is your mantra.
- You live close to where you work and play.
- You don't know how to drive. You failed driver's ed - twice. But nobody needs to know that, right?

Yes Car

- You don't live close to work and/or play.
- You've tried walking. It's either too damn cold or too stinkin' hot to get to work without looking like something the cat dragged in.
- The only public transit available doesn't give rides to muggles.
- You work crazy hours and move around a lot on your job. Monday you're out in the oil field. Tuesday you're at the supplier's office. Wednesday you're headed to the airport. And who knows where Thursday will land you, but Friday night's all about meeting everybody at The West End.

Take a look at the spending guidelines for each below.

"No Car" Spending Guidelines

Good news. You'll spend less on transportation costs than your car-bound buddies. Of course, you're probably paying an obscene amount of money for a teensy-weensy shoebox of an apartment to sleep in so it's a wash. Aim to keep your transportation costs under 10% of your gross income. You'll be mixing it up - getting around via public transit, foot, bike, or perhaps a Vespa. Scooters and motorcycles are a lot cheaper than cars, as long as you're not looking at Ducatis. But you do need to factor in the cost of leathers and helmets. Hate helmets? Whatever, but do me a favor - sign your organ donor card. And if you find yourself bumming rides, don't be "that guy." Pitch in for gas.

Your Monthly "No Car" Transportation Budget
Monthly Income = _____ x 10% = _____

Here's what you need to plan for:

Transit Pass: _____

Taxis: _____ For those late nights and foul-weather days

ZipCar: _____ For the occasional weekend out of town

**Motorcycle/Scooter
Payment:** _____ If you have a loan on it

Gas: _____ If you go the scooter/motorcycle route

Misc: _____ Repairs, insurance, license, and registration, plus cool stickers for your helmet

TOTAL: _____

"Yes Car" Spending Guidelines

To figure out your transportation budget, we've got to add up the costs of owning and driving your car. Aim for spending no more than 15 - 20% of your gross income on transportation. Remember, the more you spend on transportation, the less you have to spend on housing, food, and, well, everything else.

Your Monthly "Yes Car" Transportation Budget
Monthly Income = _____ x 15 - 20% = _____

First things first, do you have a car now? If you have a set of wheels that runs, the longer you wait to spring for the new (or newer) car, the easier it'll be on your budget. But, if you don't have a car and need one, you got three choices: buy new, buy used, or lease. Leasing, in general, is a lousy idea. It's the car dealer's way of getting you into more car than you can afford. Before you sign a lease agreement, check back on your list o' goals. I'm pretty sure renting a car for life isn't on there.

Which way to go?

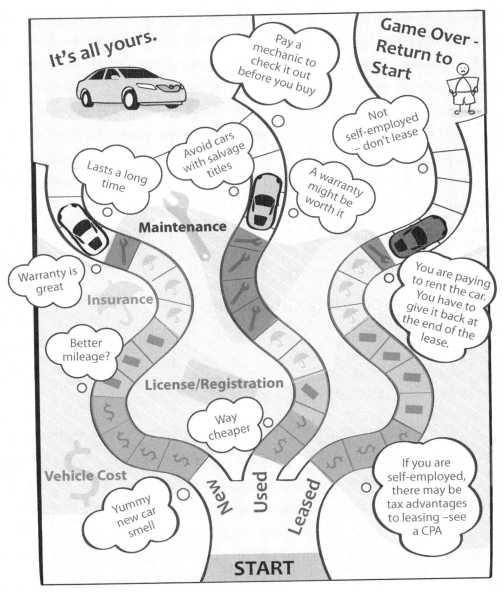

Here's what you need to plan for if you own a car:

Car Payment: _____

Gas: _____

Insurance: _____

Parking/Tolls: _____

Parking/Speeding Tickets: _*zero*_ — Parking, speeding, or whatever. Tickets for being stupid come out of your Fun Stuff budget. Seriously.

Spinners: _*zilch*_ — Did you honestly think I was going to let you budget real money to pimp your ride?

Misc: _____ — Repairs, fuzzy dice, new tires, maintenance, license/registration, bus/train, bobble-head action figure for your dashboard.

TOTAL: _____

Work backward to figure out how much car you can afford. For example, if you have $600 per month for your total transportation budget, you may need $150 for gas and another $150 for insurance, fees, and maintenance. This leaves you $300 per month, at most, for a car payment. Use an online auto-loan calculator to find out how much you can borrow to have a $300 payment. Most auto loans have three- or four-year terms, but you can stretch things out to five or six years. Longer-term loans will cost you a wee bit more in interest over the life of the loan, but they keep the payment size down. For example, a four-year $18,000 loan with a 7% interest rate has monthly payments of $431. Knock it out to six years and the payments drop to $307.

> ### Best Time to Buy
>
> **New Cars** – Late September or late December
>
> **Used Cars** – October, November or late December
>
> When new model years are around the corner you can catch a deal. It's all about inventory, baby.

Loan Amount	Term	Interest Rate	Payment
$18,000	4 years	7%	$431
$18,000	6 years	7%	$307

Total Monthly Transportation Budget: _____

Subtract all those Fixed Car Expenses: _____

TOTAL Maximum Car Payment: _____

Now that you're looking at these numbers and thinking of shelling out that money for years and years, maybe that car you're driving right now isn't so bad after all. If you already have something that runs, the longer you can wait to commit to those loan payments the better. Give it a wash and wax, some seat covers, one of those scented tree air fresheners, and it'll feel brand new.

Beware the Perils of Flashy Spending

You know those Big Spenders - always seem to have new everything - including cars. It's hard not to be envious. How do they do it? Here's the scoop. All that flashy spending leads to nasty money squabbles because they don't actually have the money. Their relationships end badly over 78% of the time.* No winners there.

Totally made that up. But we both know it's a big number.

Rounding Out the Basics

"Money can't buy happiness but it can make you awfully comfortable while you're miserable"
~ Claire Booth Luce

*a*t this point, you've got the framework for figuring out how much you can afford for rent and transportation. This is the stuff that, once you commit, you can't easily change. These items are considered necessities - things you pretty much have to have whether you want them or not. Now we want to take a look at the other necessities you've got to plan for, like food, clothing, cell phones, and such.

When it comes to food, here's the key. Meal planning. Did I just hear a groan? As if it's not bad enough that you have to plan how to spend your money, now I'm expecting you to plan what you eat, too? Yup. Skip meal planning and food will eat up your budget. Yes, eat. I'm perfectly cereal... I mean, serious. You need to set aside a certain dollar amount for eats and make it last.

The cost of food varies depending on where you live, but figure you're gonna need somewhere between 10 - 15 percent of your salary for food each month. Here's the formula:

Your Total Food Allowance Per Month

Your monthly salary _____ x 10 - 15% = _____

Making $3,000 per month? Then you've got about $320 a month for food. This includes meals out as well as groceries. I don't know whether that sounds like a lot or a little, but if you spend $8 at Chipotle or Church's Fried Chicken for lunch five days a week, you'll burn through $160 a month without getting dinner or breakfast or anything at all on weekends. Yikes. Best approach is to mix it up. Buy lunch once a week, then brown-bag it other days with zesty bologna-and-mustard-on-white-bread sandwiches. Learn to love the leftover. Cook extra portions so you can heat up those leftovers later at work or at home. Practice workplace etiquette, though. Never heat up leftover seafood in the microwave and take it back to your desk. Never.

Once you've got the food thing figured out, you need to get your clothing budget together. Clothing is a personal thing. Yes, I did just write that. And you may quote me. Here's the issue: the amount

Family of One?

You're not feeding a football team, so you will not save by buying in bulk. You do not need 24 rolls of toilet paper, a dozen monstrous muffins that you'll eat too many of, or a two-pound package of chicken-cranberry salad. Skip the Costco or Sam's membership. Ask Mom and Dad to take you in on their card once or twice a year instead.

you should spend on clothing depends. It depends on your income, your job, your preferences, and where you live. For example, folks in Tampa/St. Pete don't need winter coats, scarves, hats, or mukluks, but try living in Fargo without 'em and you'll freeze to death, dontcha know. A contractor just needs a good pair of Carhartts, maybe two; a kindergarten teacher needs a cute theme sweater for every holiday; and a fashion editor, well, you get where I'm going. Some of you need more money for clothes than others. When you're just starting out, get some basics and build on them. No one is really expecting you to look like you walked off the pages of Cosmo or GQ unless you work at Cosmo or GQ. In that case you just buy a lot of black. As far as budget, keep it under 3 - 5 percent. Make room for some fun trendy stuff, but don't build your wardrobe on one-season wonders.

Definition: Shopping

Spending money you don't have on things you don't need and can't afford. If your favorite bumper sticker says "Born to Shop," be smart about it. Master the art of buying and selling. Buy on sale, sell on Craigslist or eBay. Set a budget and do your homework to stretch those shopping dollars. Make sure what you're buying is worth it. You don't want to end up.....

Your cell phone is another item that goes in the "necessities" section of your spending plan. Some of you may be lucky enough to continue riding the family-plan wave for a while. The rest of you need to do some smart shopping. When buying a cell phone, experts recommend you make sure you thoroughly understand the fees, taxes, service charges, regulatory charges, administrative charges, access charges, usage charges, overage surcharges, roaming charges, and penalties applicable to your specific service plan. Yeah, good luck with that.

Necessities also include the broad "personal care" category. This includes everything from haircuts and dry cleaning to gym memberships and fees for fitness classes. Warning: Your budget for personal care items is only 3 - 5 percent of your monthly income, so figure out how to make the most of it. Stretch those haircuts out an extra week (or two) but don't wait until you look like Hagrid (please). Shop for clothing that does not need to be dry cleaned. If you're not even sure what dry cleaning is then this probably isn't an issue. Gym memberships can be pricey - shop around for the best deal. Get creative. Consider getting a side gig as a personal trainer, spinning guru, or high priestess of Zumba to get your fitness for free. Here's the personal care budget formula:

Your Total Personal Care Allowance Per Month

Your monthly salary _____ **x 3 - 5% =** _____

Donations and gifts are the final category we want to touch on for your basic spending. There is no set percentage for this category because, well, it's a personal thing. Some folks automatically donate 10 percent of their income to charity. This is known as 'tithing'. Others donate as they can or feel like it; still others don't at all. If you don't want to, as the Dude would say, "that's your opinion, man." But I say make an effort to donate something - it's good karma.

Gift-giving. So many people get out of control at Santa time that they spend the first half of the next year recovering. Don't let that be you. Set aside a certain amount each month for gifts - birthdays, Christmas, Hanukkah, Kwanzaa, or any other traditions you've got. Stay within that budget. If things are really tight, think of gifts that don't cost money. I'm not talking about the macaroni ornament or the ceramic, uh, paperweight you made in third grade art class. I'm talking about changing the oil in your sister's car. Making Mom an awesome playlist. Giving your brother and sister-in-law a night out by babysitting their little ankle-biters.

Making beef-jerky. I don't actually know how you make beef jerky, by the way. I'm not sure I want to know. All I'm saying is that it's an idea.

Quiz: Gift-Giving

You're trying to save money to buy a car and pay off your student loans. Which of the following is an appropriate gift for your best buddy?

A. Front-row seats to an NHL game for the two of you.
B. Season One of Jersey Shore, the complete collection, on DVD.
C. A copy of this book.
D. A belt you made out of bottle caps from his favorite beer.

Answers

A. Wrong. Wait until you're making big bucks and this is a business expense.
B. Wrong. You didn't read the question. We're talking about a gift for a friend. Friends don't let friends watch Jersey Shore.
C. Correct. This idea is genius.
D. I'll accept this one. Nice, environmentally sensitive gesture that shows you care.

⚕ *Living is Risky Business*

"When in doubt, don't."
~ Ben Franklin

*E*very day there are risks you take - insurance protects you from being financially destroyed by these risks. Yawn. The good news is, there are just a few types you need when you are starting out, so this chapter is mercifully short. Please don't skip it though. Mistakes here are one of the most frequent causes of financial ruin. And we don't want that.

Health Insurance

Now *this* is a fun topic. Not. So let's cover it quickly. You gotta have health insurance. Someway, somehow. Do not go without it. Here's the short list of options:

1. **You are covered by health insurance at your new job.** Some employers cover the full cost, while many expect employees to kick in a little bit. If there are multiple insurance plans offered by your employer, you need to compare the costs and benefits. If you are healthy and don't tend to go to the doctor much, you can save money by choosing a high-deductible plan (HDHP) or an HMO. The deductible represents the medical expenses you pay before the

insurance company starts to pay. In other words, if you have a $2,000 deductible, you'll pay the first $2,000 in medical expenses each year before your insurance policy starts to pay. If your employer offers an HDHP, you may also have the option of setting up a Health Savings Account (HSA). An HSA is a tax-deductible savings account you have to pay for your medical expenses, such as prescriptions, doctor's visits, medical equipment, and health tests. This is a good thing - so set it up. HMO stands for Health Maintenance Organization. You don't get to choose your doctor when using an HMO, but if you don't go much anyway, so what? No big deal if it saves you money. If you have certain doctors you see regularly, though, and you want to keep them, you'll probably be better off choosing a Preferred Provider Organization (PPO). If all this alphabet soup has you confused, then here's the short answer - if you are healthy, pick the cheapest coverage offered. If you have health issues, spring for the more expensive option.

> ### Short on Beer Money?
> ### 5 Tips to Save $$ on Medical Costs
>
> 1. Quit smoking.
> 2. Don't super-size yourself or your Coke®.
> 3. Go easy on the high fructose corn syrup. I know, easier said than done.
> 4. Drink lots of water - but use a refillable bottle, for crying out loud.
> 5. Scale back on the beer.

2. **You can stay covered on your parents' insurance until you are 26.** This is an excellent choice if they have a family plan that costs the same whether you're on it or not. Free is good.

3. **Sign up for insurance through the Health Insurance Marketplace.** www.HealthCare.gov. Under the Affordable Care Act most folks are required to have health insurance or pay a fine. I don't want you paying fines! The good news is if your income is less than $45,960 there may be tax credits that lower the cost. Depending on your budget and your insurance needs, you choose a platinum, gold, silver, or bronze plan. Bronze gets you a high deductible plan so if you're healthy you can save by going that route. If you're not so healthy or you're incredibly clumsy, go with gold or platinum. The premiums

are higher but the insurance covers more out of pocket costs when you cut your hand while slicing a bagel for the seventh time. If you're under 30 you can also choose a low-cost catastrophic plan. Any of these keeps you from paying the fine and gives you a place to go when you're sick. Not sure how you'll afford it? Well, there's always money in the banana stand.

Pay Me Now or Pay Me Later

Louie goes skiing. He doesn't take a lesson because, well, you know Louie. Anyway, he french fried when he was supposed to pizza and ended up having a bad time. The average cost of a 2-day hospital stay can run **$20,000**. With no insurance, Louie will have to set up a payment plan. How does $400/month until infinity* sound?

Eddie was snowboarding when Louie crashed into him. For 2 days he's stuck in the hospital bed next to Louie but at least he had insurance. Eddie has catastrophic insurance that costs him $150/mo. He'll owe the full deductible of $6,350 (ouch!) but that's a lot less than $20k. Plus, now that he's met his annual deductible, he doesn't have to pay anything for other medical treatments for the year.

Well, that's what 5 years of payments will feel like.

4. **Purchase an individual policy.** Income too high for those sweet, sweet tax credits? Yeah, mine is too. Not by much, though. Anyway, don't worry. You still have options. Go directly to insurance companies for quotes, work with an insurance agent or broker, or check out online health insurance companies. You can go through the Marketplace, too. Compare costs from different sources to get the best deal. Sadly, there are no Groupons or Living Social deals for this stuff.

5. **Marry someone who has great health insurance.** No, I'm not really serious. This would be weird.

6. **Sign up for Medicaid.** If you qualify, go for it. Just get something!

Life Insurance

BASE jumping. Breath-hold diving. Free climbing. If you participate in any of these activities, buy a boatload of five-year term life insurance and name me as the beneficiary. Check the cover of this book to make sure you spell my name right. Thanks!

Everybody else - skip it. That was easy, wasn't it? You don't need life insurance until you have someone depending on your income for their support. You can make an exception if your Alpha Sigma brother Louie just got a job selling life insurance and you want to help a brother out. Buy a small policy. Really small. Oh, and make him buy you dinner.

Disability Insurance

Not the cheeriest of topics, for sure, but statistically speaking, you are more likely to become disabled through an accident or illness than you are to die prematurely. This is true even if you never go BASE jumping, breath-hold diving, free climbing, or participate in anything riskier than the occasional foray into World of Warcraft. I know, crazy, right? But think about it - if you become disabled, you probably can't work. At the very least, your employment options will be seriously limited. And yet, you would still need to eat and live somewhere. You would probably need help with medical bills. This is why you want to have disability insurance.

If you have disability insurance as an option at work, take it. There are two kinds: short-term and long-term. You want both. If this is not an option through work, see if it's available through one of your professional associations. You can also try getting a quote online, but you'll probably need to wait until you've been in the working world a few years to qualify.

Auto Insurance

How's your driving record? Got any speeding tickets? If you haven't already, now is a really good time to develop some safe driving habits. In fact, it's an excellent time. The more tickets and accidents on your record, the more your insurance costs. Why? Because insurance companies aren't stupid. They know young drivers are riskier than older ones, and if you already have a lousy record, you're proving it.

If you do have a good driving record, your insurance will be cheaper. Pink drivers are cheaper than blue drivers up to age 25. The age and type of car you're driving makes a big difference, too. A four-door sedan will cost less to insure than a two-door sports car. Likewise, an older car will cost less to insure than a newer one, because it's less valuable. That is, unless you're driving daddy's hand-me-down Jaguar X-J6. If that's the case, he's probably paying your insurance, so you can just skip this section.

Quiz: Which vehicle costs the least to insure?

A. Dodge Viper
B. Ford Shelby
C. Jeep Wrangler
D. Audi R8

Answer: C. The Jeep Wrangler costs roughly half as much as the others to insure.

Your auto insurance policy is actually a bundle of up to six different kinds of insurance: bodily injury liability, medical payments (aka Personal Injury Protection, aka PIP), property damage liability, collision, comprehensive, and uninsured motorists coverage. All on one convenient little piece of paper. Where you live, how much you drive, and the kind of car you drive determine whether you need an insurance policy that covers you for all six or not. Shop around for your auto insurance. Get quotes from a few insurance companies, but keep in mind that the cheapest premium may not be the best deal. Check the reviews on the company to make sure they don't suck when it comes to paying claims. Ideally, you want to find an insurance rep who will explain the different types of coverage and offer ways to keep your insurance costs down.

Join AAA. It costs less than $50 per year for a basic policy. Use it once and it's paid for itself. AAA will come change your flat tire, help you get in your car if you locked the keys in it (who does that?), bring gas if you run out, tow your car for repairs - all kinds of stuff. It's especially handy if you're stuck driving your uncle's '86 Ford Fiesta - kind of rare, but not impossible. AAA also offers auto insurance, so you can compare their price with other quotes you get.

Renter's Insurance

When you're renting, you don't care about the building. I mean, you care a little, but if there's a broken window, you call the landlord. Leaky shower, ditto. But what you do care about is your own stuff. That nice sound system. The Italian road bike. The MacBook Air. Let's face it - you probably like having your own clothes. So, you need to have a renter's insurance policy. The price depends on the value of your valuables, but it's generally pretty cheap. Plan on $5-15 a month. In case of fire, flood, or theft, your renter's insurance policy reimburses you for your losses, so you can replace what was destroyed. Keeps you from having to walk around in public wearing donated jorts. So worth it.

⑩ The "R" Word

"Don't go around saying the world owes you a living. The world owes you nothing. It was here first."
~ Mark Twain

*Y*ou've graduated from college and are working full time. It's great. You love it. You could do this every day of your life. Forever. And ever. Or, perhaps you'd like to consider the possibility of not working at some point. Instead of working full time, you'd like to be able to play full time. Either way, let me lay out your options:

1. Work until the day you drop dead.
2. Buy Powerball tickets and hope you are the 1 in 1,000,000,000 that wins.
3. Marry rich. I mean, marry someone with buckets of money, not necessarily someone named Rich.
4. Inherit a fortune from your long-lost uncle who happened to be a Nigerian prince. According to the email you received, all you have to

do is wire $2,500 to process the estate.

5. Save and invest a portion of what you earn so that someday you don't have to work if you don't feel like it.

Let's take a look at each of these. The first option might be appealing, might not. This is the go-to option in most third-world countries and communist regimes. It's also not completely unheard of here in the USA., but it's probably not the option of choice. Second one is pretty unlikely. Go ahead and buy a lottery ticket once in a while when you're feeling lucky, but this doesn't count as a real plan. Plus, have you heard how messed up most lottery winners get? It's not all it's cracked up to be. Seriously. Moving on to number 3. It could happen. I still think you need a little more of an actual plan. Number 4 might be real, but which one of those emails is legit? And how come your mom never mentioned an uncle in Nigeria? Of course, if number 2 happens, you'll probably discover all kinds of friends and relatives you never knew you had. Realistically, all this leads us to option number 5. But you knew that.

The easiest way to reach the day when all you do is play is to sock your money away. The sooner you start socking away money, the sooner you'll be financially free to do what you want: continue working full time, switch to playing full time, or order up the combo platter.

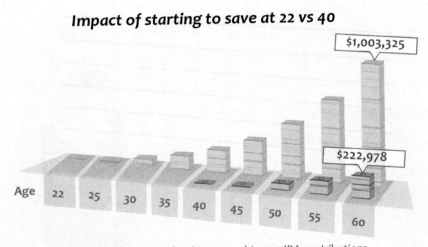

Impact of starting to save at 22 vs 40

$1,003,325

$222,978

Age 22 25 30 35 40 45 50 55 60

Start and end age of making annual $5,500 IRA contributions

Individual Retirement Account

What to do when you're 22? Open a Roth IRA—an Individual Retirement Account. This is an investment account for *your* money to pay for *your* freedom later. The best place to do this is at a brokerage firm so you can invest the money. However, most brokerage firms have $1,000 minimums. If you don't have that yet, head to your local bank and buy a certificate of deposit, known as a CD, to open your IRA. The CD pays a little more interest than a savings account. It's not much, but getting started is what matters most. The longer you wait, the greater the odds are that you'll end up old and poor and bitter. We don't want that.

Once the Roth IRA is open, add to it each month faithfully. You can put in up to $5,500 each year (as of 2014), and this should be your target. If you start at a bank, once you have over $1,000, move your money over to a brokerage firm.

Roth IRA vs. Traditional IRA

When you are young, you want to put as much money as you can into a Roth IRA for several reasons. The basic difference between the Roth IRA and the Traditional IRA is that you already paid tax on the money you put in a Roth, so it will grow tax free. Later, when you retire and use the money to live on, there are no taxes to pay—even if your investments have doubled or tripled! A Traditional IRA, on the other hand, has money that has not been taxed. You get to take a deduction on your taxes for funding a Traditional IRA, which is cool, but when it's time to take money out to live on, you have to pay taxes on all the money you put in plus all your earnings. If your IRA investments triple, you'll pay tax on all those earnings. Unless you are modeling with Elite or you're a first-round draft pick in the NFL, it's likely you are going to be in a lower tax bracket in your 20s than you will be later on. Even though you don't get to deduct these contributions on your tax return, you will be richer faster by putting your money in the Roth IRA.

The 411 on the 401(k)/403(b)

Next, enroll in your 401(k) at work. What a catchy name, you say. Let's face it, accounting and tax people do not have a flair for marketing. 401(k) is the section of the U.S. Tax Code that describes how workers can save money through their employer. If you work for a government, school, hospital, or a non-profit, you might have a TSA, a 403(b), a 401(a), or a 457 plan. For now, you can think of them all as being pretty much the same thing. Every few years you'll see a new flavor rolled out. Anyway, the idea is you sign up to set aside some of your salary for later. Not all employers offer these plans, and some make you wait up to a year to enroll, but as soon as you are eligible, sign up. Just like the IRA plans, there are Roth and Traditional options. If you have an option for a Roth 401(k), take it. You will become so wealthy so fast it'll make your head spin. Not really, but do it anyway. If you don't have the Roth option, sign up for whatever saving option is available.

You can set aside (defer) up to $17,500 of your income each year (as of 2014) to your 401(k). Divide this amount by the annual number of paychecks to figure out how much you want taken out each pay period. For example, if you get paid every two weeks, you have 26 paychecks a year. To maximize your deferrals, you should sign up to have $673 of each paycheck put into your 401(k). Are you gagging? Sorry about that. If you can't swing the full amount, start with a smaller amount like $250 per paycheck or 10% per paycheck, whatever you can handle, and increase it every year.

Free money. Ah, I figured I'd catch your attention with that. Who doesn't like free money? In the 401(k) world, you can get free money. It's called the employer match. Many employers want to encourage you to save for your future – love them! They'll offer a match – you agree to put some of your paycheck into your 401(k) and they'll match what you put in – up to a point. Not all employers offer a match but if yours does, take it! Always max the match. So easy.

What Investments Do I Choose for My IRAs and 401(k)?

When you're just starting out, your accounts won't be very big. Not many dollars to divvy up. Stick with easy and choose a "Target Date" fund. These funds all have a year at the end of their names, like Target Date 2045, Freedom Fund 2050, or Target Fund ∞, which represents the year you're thinking you'll be able to stop working. The fund managers spread your dollars across various investments based on how long it will be before you plan to access the money (i.e. the target date). Some goes into stocks, some into bonds, and some into a combination of things like real estate, pork bellies, jujubes, gold, or other commodities that allow the money you invest to grow over time.

What about Social Security?

What about it? Oh, right—yes, you have money deducted from your paychecks that goes into Social Security. And your employer tosses some in there on your behalf, too. Someday when you are very old, you may be eligible to receive monthly checks from the Social Security Agency that you can use however you want. Cash those checks and spend the money on oatmeal, Wednesday night Bingo at the Senior Center, or sensible shoes.

If your lifestyle expectations are higher, and, man, I hope they are, then you need to take matters into your own hands. It's YOYO—you're on your own.* Start saving money now.

That's YOYO – not YOLO. Nobody says YOLO anymore, do they?

11 T@xe$

> *"In this world nothing can be said to be certain, except death and taxes."*
> *~ Our man, Ben Franklin*

You have a job. Your job pays you money. This money is income. If you have income, Uncle Sam gets a cut. Take the quiz:

Quiz: Which of the following is/are NOT income?

A. Your employer pays you a $3,000 salary every month.

B. At Eddie's Vegas bachelor party you win $1,575 by putting it all down on Red 19.

C. The bank pays you $1.29 in interest on your savings account.

D. Grandma Betty gives you $13,000 because she loves you and you are the only grandchild who ever writes thank-you notes.

E. You win $500 for third place in a science-fiction writing contest.

F. You received a $3,000 scholarship that you used to pay for your rent the last semester of school.

G. You sell 10 shares of Google stock and make $312 on the deal.

Answer: D is the only one that is not considered income. No income = no tax due. Be nice to Grandma Betty and make sure you write that thank-you note!

The list of things that are considered income is much longer than this, but you get the idea. Piddly little amounts of income owe piddly little amounts of tax, but you need to let the IRS know what you earned. Otherwise, they get pretty bent out of shape about it. Steep penalties and jail time are the tools they use to get their point across. Nothing cool about tax evasion. Most states collect their own income tax, too, but if you live in Alaska, Florida, Nevada, New Hampshire, South Dakota, Tennessee, Texas, Washington, or Wyoming, you're off the hook on this.

To file your tax return, use one of the free or cheap online tools available. Keep in mind that you have to pay taxes, but there's no need to pay *extra*. Here are a few things to consider that may reduce what you owe:

1. **Student Loan Interest.** If it's your student loan and not your parents', the interest you pay can be deducted from your income. The limits are pretty low on the amount you're allowed to deduct each year. Write your congressman. Get that limit raised.
2. **FSA/HSA accounts.** Your employer may offer a Flexible Spending Account or a medical insurance plan with a Health Savings Account. If these are available to you, take advantage of them. This reduces your taxable income.
3. **Fund your retirement accounts.** This one's a little tricky, so check back on the previous chapter ("The 'R' Word") to see what option fits your situation best.
4. **Make babies.** Just kidding! You do get a tax deduction for each dependent, but wait until later for that. Please. Speaking of dependents, check with your parents before you file. If they paid for more than half of your support for the year, they'll probably claim you as their dependent, so you can't claim yourself. That would be double-dipping and the IRS says don't do that.
5. **Make less money.** Duh.

If your situation is complicated, spend a couple hundred bucks to talk to a Certified Public Accountant (CPA). For example, if you're starting your own business or working as an independent contractor (receiving a Form 1099 instead of a W2 showing your earnings), then you have to pay your own taxes each quarter because you don't have an employer taking care of it for you. A CPA will help you figure out how much you'll owe for income tax, self-employment tax, unemployment tax, and any other taxes that might come up. He'll also show you how to file each quarter. And all this keeps you out of jail, which, again, is cool. If you have income from a trust, a settlement, or stock options, meet with a CPA before the end of the year to know what you'll owe. You don't want to get to April 15th and find out that killer sound system you bought in February needs to go up on Craigslist to pay your tax bill, do you?

Don't Mess with the IRS

Think you can just ignore taxes? Bad idea. It may take the IRS a while to catch up to you, but time is on their side. If you don't pay what you owe on time, that money accrues interest and penalties at a pretty steep rate.

Just ask singer Willie Nelson. In 1990, the IRS sent him notice saying he owed $6.5 million in taxes for income earned between 1978 and 1982. Oh, and he also owed $10.2 million in penalties and interest for late payment. Ouch. He didn't have the money, so the IRS auctioned off everything he owned as payment. And then, he hit the road (again) and sang his butt off to raise the rest. Fans and friends helped by buying his belongings at the IRS estate sale and giving them back to him. Not exactly what I'd want to have "Always on My Mind."

12 The Fun Stuff

> *"I want an Oompa-Loompa! screamed Veruca."*
> *~ Roald Dahl, Charlie and the Chocolate Factory*

Quiz: Which one doesn't belong?

A. Baseball tickets
B. Friday night happy hour
C. Weekend in Napa
D. Lift tickets
E. Volleyball league fee

Answer: Tricked you! These all belong. To one degree or another, they're all considered "Fun Stuff." These are the good things in life.

Finally! The fun stuff. I bet you were starting to worry that we'd never get here. But you can relax now, because we're going to talk about spending money on play. This is often called "discretionary spending" because you're supposed to show discretion and not spend it until you've taken care of all your other financial obligations. That does a pretty good job of taking the fun out of it, doesn't it? But, don't worry—we've already covered that, so now we can enjoy planning your playtime.

Traveling With Friends:

Getting Everyone to Pay Their Fair Share

Ever traveled with someone who turned out to be such a bum that you never wanted to see him again? Me neither. But I've heard about people like that. Money squabbles have been known to ruin great vacations. Here's how to avoid them.

1. *Agree on the general budget before you go. Are we talking KOA campground or the Four Seasons?*
2. *Agree to have everyone split group expenses but pay their own individual expenses. If Chelsea insists she needs a $250 seaweed wrap boiling lava massage, great— that's her thing, not yours.*
3. *Have each person keep track of what they spend for the group before and during the trip. Maybe one person picked up the dinner tab, while someone else paid for the condo.*
4. *At the end of the trip, add up everyone's group expenses. Divide that by the number of people in the group. That's the amount each person owes.*
5. *Those who paid less for group expenses repay those who paid extra, so that everyone's even.*

Here's an example: Four friends go for a beach weekend. Ali pays $300 for the condo rental. Benny drives everyone and spends $80 on gas. He also picks up the dinner tab ($100). Cara spends $200 on groceries for the other meals. Dean pays for nothing but he makes everybody laugh.

Total trip cost: $300 + 80 + 100 + 200 = $680
Cost per person = $170
Dean owes $170. Humor's great, but that doesn't get him out of paying.
This means Cara is owed $30, Benny is owed $10, and Ali is owed $130.
Dean pays each of them their respective amount (which, if you didn't catch, adds up to his $170) and everybody's all square. And they'll probably want to go again!

Since there are more things to spend money on than there is money, you need to be selective about how you use these dollars. Vacation, recreation, hobbies, and entertainment are just a few examples of "Fun Stuff" categories. Earmark a certain amount each month for these and, as specific opportunities come up, you've got the money to pay for them. One month it might be Cubs tickets or a wine tasting, while another month it might be a beach weekend—so just try to nail down an average per month you think you can afford after all the other bills have been paid.

The biggest budget busters are probably going to be weddings. Not yours necessarily. I'm talking about the weddings of friends and family members. It may not happen right away, but within the first couple years out of school, you'll find yourself boogie-ing from one wedding to another. Not a problem if they're in your backyard—not your literal backyard, silly, I mean if they're held somewhere nearby. Otherwise, you need to pay for plane tickets and hotels. If you're in the party, the tux rental or bridesmaid dress and shoes come into play. And you put on bachelor parties. Or bachelorette parties. Bridal showers. Did I mention the gifts? If you've got a large circle of close friends, you'll need to do some serious saving to fund your participation in these events. Plan for them, so you can focus on these good times and memories with good friends instead of the wallet damage. And sometimes, sadly, you'll have to say no. That sunset ceremony overlooking the Aegean on the cliffs of Hydra sounds absolutely amazing, but if you don't have an extra $5k to spare, you'll just have to enjoy the pictures on Facebook.

Body art, lip plumping, grills, piercings, and any other... um... cosmetic enhancements go in the Fun Stuff section. Yes, this is the rule even though these things are excruciating to get. Ironic, isn't it? I know you were kinda thinking they're basic necessities, but that's not how it works. You need to save up for them, just like anything else. And if you're getting a tattoo, do the rest of us a favor—do your homework and get a good one. Work with a talented tattoo artist. I try to appreciate a cool tattoo as much as the next person, but nobody, and I do mean nobody, likes looking at an ugly tattoo.

Tattoo removal, on the other hand, absolutely goes in the Necessities—Personal Care" category. If you happen to be in a career where that serpent wrapped around your neck dampens your earning potential, the cost of getting it removed

Budgeting Your Body Art

Note: Prices vary – wildly – so the numbers here are mid-range. Not sure you really want to go for the 'best deal' with this kind of thing.

Botox
$400
Beware the shiny forehead

Monroe Piercing
$55
Intimidating, tres cool, but incredibly painful.

Nose Piercing
$40
Trendy but make sure inside stem is really short or else it looks like you forgot to wipe your nose. Seriously

Lip Plumping
$475

⬆ Boob Job
$10,000
Cost to get implants

⬇ Boob Job
$6,500
Cost to remove implants

Bellybutton Piercing
$30
Nice and sparkly. Great on the beach. Covers up well so the office doesn't need to know.

⬆ Small Tattoo
$75
Easy for something memorable, small enough to avoid distraction.

⬇ Laser Removal
$500
Effective but incredibly painful. Like being covered in hot grease.

Henna Tattoo
$30
Lasts only 1-3 weeks, great if you want to remember a moment. Nice way to flip out Grandma yet not get written out of her will.

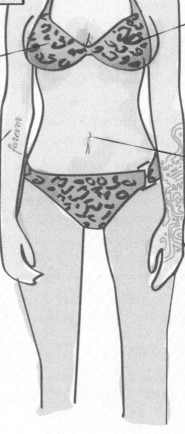

forever

Eyebrow Piercing
$40
Intimidating – definitely making a statement. Make sure it's the statement you want to make.

Ear Gauges
$35
Gives you an edgy look but also leaves your earlobes looking like ABC gum. Consider faux gauges instead if you want to have a career as something other than a sandwich artist or rapper wannabe.

Accent Tattoo
$500
Great for cementing an image. May not gel w/your choice of career but that's what gloves and turtlenecks are for, right?

To Repair
$1,000
Cost of surgery

Dermabrasion
$1,500
Literally sanding away the skin, can be effective but also very painful for the skin and nerve endings

Large Tattoo
$1,500
Talk about making a statement! Time consuming and painful to have done. Certainly will make Mom & Dad rethink that hissy fit they threw when you came home sporting the emo haircut.

Fade-Away Tattoo
$500
The ink penetrates fewer layers of skin, so it fades over time. Smart choice for those who love 'em and leave 'em.

Intense Pulsed Light Therapy Removal
$1,500
Less painful than laser removal

Care category. If you happen to be in a career where that serpent wrapped around your neck dampens your earning potential, the cost of getting it removed pays for itself pretty quickly. Did you know that half of all people who get tattoos eventually try to have them removed? I did not make that up. It's a genuine fact.

Tats and Monroes aside, you decide what's important to you. Don't worry about whether it makes sense to someone else (like me, for instance). If it makes you happy and you can afford it, then that's where your money belongs.

⑬ Putting It All Together

"Beware of little expenses. A small leak will sink a great ship."
~ Ben Franklin

Y ou've got all the pieces—now let's get that spending plan done. We'll use the worksheet below and your trusty pencil to knock it out. Get some good music on. That means no Taylor Swift—seriously. None of that dub-step crap either.

Scan the list of spending categories. Cross out any that don't apply so you don't freak out. Simple, right? Tackle the plan in three parts.

First, if you have one, grab a recent paystub. If not, you'll have to estimate the amounts deducted for taxes and benefits. Enter this in the worksheet. It's rough looking at your net income. You were probably still trying to figure out why Pluto isn't really a planet after all and now you discover how little you have to live on each month after all that time in school. If you aren't funding your 401(k) or other retirement plan yet, make a note to sign up for it as soon as possible. On that line, put in the amount you plan to defer to it. Do not ignore it.

Next, add the "Necessities," aka the basics. Again, estimate where needed. If you're still in your grace period for student loans, use this time to build your emergency fund. When those loans hit, you've got to stay on top of them until they're fully paid off, so get the emergency fund out of the way. And hey, if you don't have any loans or debt, go ahead and smile.

And now, the glorious Fun Stuff. All the good things in life come into play here: entertainment, dining out, recreation, and don't forget vacation. Add your own hobbies and activities plus the goals you prioritized back when we started. Of course, I do need to warn you—since these happen after you've fulfilled all your financial obligations, this is where you'll probably have the biggest challenge in making your plan work.

My Spending Plan   Today's Date: _____

	Estimate	Actual	
Gross Income			
Your Paycheck Deductions			
Taxes			FWH, SWH, FICA, etc
Retirement Plans			401(k), 403(b), 457 deferrals
Benefits			Health Insurance Premiums
Net Income			Your take-home pay
Necessities			
Savings			
Roth IRA			
Rent			
Food			Includes groceries & restaurants
Clothing			
Personal Care			
Medical			
Gifts/Donations			

	Estimate	Actual	
Transportation			
Loan Payments			
Utilities			
Cell Phone			
Insurance			
Other			
The Fun Stuff			
Entertainment			Baseball tickets, concerts, movies
Recreation			Ski tickets, camping permits
Vacation			
Other			
Total Spending			
Net Income —Spending			

How'd you do? How does it look when you subtract all your expenses from your net income? Do you have gobs of money left over, or are you not even close? Yeah, I figured you'd probably come up short the first go-around, but no need to wig out. This happens to pretty much everybody except for certain accounting grads who have a mutated fun gene in their DNA.* So sad.

What to do if there's not enough income to match your outgo? You have to scale back or figure out how to make more. Choose one or two categories and try to do with less—maybe it's time to carpool, pack your lunch, or scale back on dining out. Drink domestic instead of imported beer. Quit smoking. Forget the swank penthouse—find cheaper housing. Instead of the fancy gym, hit the local rec center. You can't afford to spend a lot on clothing or cars if you have credit card or student loan debt. Lather, rinse, repeat. Keep whittling until you've got

*I think I remember reading something about this in The Onion. Either that or I just made it up.

a spending plan that works. Be selective and get creative. There's a reason we tackled this in pencil, not pen. It takes a few tries and some give-and-take to have a plan that will work for you. But it's definitely worth doing. Do it now, while life is relatively simple, and it will become such a habit that you'll be healthy, wealthy, and wise before you know it.

Bank Fees & Overdraft Charges

Overdraft charges can be as high as $35. Per charge. Such a rip-off. These are as bad as parking tickets, and like parking tickets, they are completely avoidable. Think about what you could do with that money. If you are earning $30,000 a year, it takes you almost half a day to earn the after-tax money to pay that. Wouldn't you rather spend that on a couple large pepperoni pizzas and a six-pack, or maybe a nice pedicure?

Leave a buffer in your checking account so you don't overdraw. One easy way to do this is to give it a false bottom. Put a hundred dollars in there that you'll pretend doesn't exist.

Also, sign up with your bank to have your debit card turned down if there isn't enough in the account at the time of a transaction. Opt out of the automatic overdraft. If you find you're getting turned down when you try to use your debit card, leave the card at home and switch to a cash-only basis to get a handle on your spending.

Once you have your plan laid out, you need to track it. For this task, you can use a budget app on your smartphone, a spreadsheet, or budgeting software program. Look at your bank's website to see what tools they offer. There are many free money-tracking options available (with new shipments arriving daily!), so find one you like and run with it.

Get in the habit of paying attention to your spending. You don't run out of gas all the time, do you? You have a gas gauge and you look at it every time you get behind the wheel. Make it a practice to check your spending regularly and you won't end up wasting precious dollars. And that leaves you more money for fun stuff. And life will be good.

Making Change

"... what you learn today, for no reason at all, will help you discover all the wonderful secrets of tomorrow."
~ Norton Juster, The Phantom Tollbooth

*Y*ou're finished! Congratulations! You've got the know-how to manage your money. And you've got your plan. It's time to ditch the water wings and dive in to your future. But first, thumb back through the book. Write down the five tasks you need to take care of right away:

1. _____
2. _____
3. _____
4. _____
5. _____

Refer to your plan regularly, and track your progress. A spending plan is not a one-shot deal. Maintaining a spending plan is one of those things you check regularly from here on out. Like Facebook. Celebrate those successes—like when your emergency fund is in place or you've saved the money you need for your trip to Tibet. As you accomplish goals, make sure you add new ones. That's why you're working after all. Check **www.CoinInTheBank.com** for ideas on how to keep it real, keep it fun, and stay engaged.

And, always, live by the Platinum Rule.

The Platinum Rule
SPEND LESS THAN YOU MAKE.

Wait!

No doubt you are sad to have reached the end of this book but that doesn't mean we're through! Keep your financial good times rolling by heading straight to:

www.coininthebank.com

Here you'll find answers to your financial questions, tools and worksheets to download, up-to-date information on ways to make your money grow, and, of course, plenty of laughs.

About the Author

Judy McNary, CFP®, owns a fee-only financial planning firm and thoroughly enjoys helping each of her clients craft their financial futures. A parent of three adult children in their twenties, she believes life is more fun when you and your money get off to a great start.

When not melding client dreams with numbers, Judy relaxes by swimming with the sharks as a volunteer diver for the Downtown Aquarium in Denver. Putting her money where her heart is, she pledges through 1% for the Planet to support Project Aware, a nonprofit dedicated to protecting our oceans.

www.McNaryFinancial.com
www.CoinInTheBank.com

About the Illustrator

Jenna Kusmierek's passion for art and design started at an early age. She completed her first oil painting at age 12 and mastered Adobe Creative Suite by age 16. Jenna is now the owner and lead designer of JMK Design Studio, a creative agency and web design firm in Denver, CO.

Jenna primarily works with small businesses, start-ups, and non-profits on projects and causes that she feels passionately about. She is thrilled to help the next generation develop the skills they need to get coin in the bank.

www.JMKDesignStudio.com

CPSIA information can be obtained
at www.ICGtesting.com
Printed in the USA
LVOW01s1251110116

468994LV00011B/52/P

9 780988 851900